Great Women in History

Harriet Tubman

by Erin Edison

Consulting Editor: Gail Saunders-Smith, PhD

Consultant: Dr. Brie Swenson Arnold
Assistant Professor of History
Coe College, Cedar Rapids, Iowa

CAPSTONE PRESS
a capstone imprint

Pebble Books are published by Capstone Press,
1710 Roe Crest Drive, North Mankato, Minnesota 56003.
www.capstonepub.com

Library of Congress Cataloging-in-Publication Data
Edison, Erin.
   Harriet Tubman / by Erin Edison.
      p. cm.—(Pebble books. Great women in history)
   Includes bibliographical references and index.
   ISBN 978-1-62065-072-1 (library binding)
   ISBN 978-1-62065-859-8 (paperback)
   ISBN 978-1-4765-1627-1 (eBook PDF)
   1. Tubman, Harriet, 1820?-1913—Juvenile literature. 2. Slaves—United States—
Biography—Juvenile literature. 3. African American women—Biography—Juvenile
literature. 4. African Americans—Biography—Juvenile literature. 5. Underground
Railroad—Juvenile literature. I. Title.
   E444.T82E44 2013
   973.7′115092—dc23
   [B]
                                                              2012033623

Note to Parents and Teachers

The Great Women in History set supports national social studies
standards related to people and culture. This book describes and
illustrates Harriet Tubman. The images support early readers in
understanding the text. The repetition of words and phrases helps
early readers learn new words. This book also introduces early
readers to subject-specific vocabulary words, which are defined
in the Glossary section. Early readers may need assistance to read
some words and to use the Table of Contents, Glossary, Read More,
Internet Sites, and Index sections of the book.

Printed in the United States of America in Stevens Point, Wisconsin.
092012   006937WZS13

Table of Contents

Early Life. 5
Escaping Slavery 11
Life's Work 15
Remembering Harriet 21

Glossary 22
Read More 23
Internet Sites. 23
Index 24

1820s

born

Early Life

Harriet Tubman was a brave woman
who helped slaves find freedom.
She was born in the 1820s
in Dorchester County, Maryland.
Harriet and her family were slaves.
They were not free to choose
their jobs or homes.

1820s   late 1820s

born   begins working

As a slave, Harriet started working

when she was about 5 years old.

She was sent away from her parents.

She had to clean her owner's home

and take care of his children.

As she got older, she worked

in the fields.

1820s
born

late 1820s
begins
working

Most slaves lived in the southern United States. In northern states, slavery was against the law. Some slaves tried to escape to the North.

slaves escaping north

1820s — born

late 1820s — begins working

1849 — escapes to Pennsylvania

Escaping Slavery

Harriet dreamed of escape.

In 1849 Harriet made her dream come true. She walked 90 miles (145 kilometers) to Pennsylvania and became free. But Harriet worried about her family and friends. She wanted to help them.

1820s
born

late 1820s
begins
working

1849
escapes to
Pennsylvania

1850s
leads people on
Underground Railroad

Harriet became part of
the Underground Railroad.
Escaping slaves used this system
of safe houses. They secretly
traveled from one house to another.
Using boats, wagons, and trains,
Harriet led people north.

1820s	late 1820s	1849	1850s
born	begins working	escapes to Pennsylvania	leads people on Underground Railroad

Life's Work

Harriet helped many slaves
escape during the 1850s.
She led about 300 people
along the Underground Railroad.
Harriet's work was dangerous.
Slave owners paid people
to try to capture her.

 Harriet (far left)

1820s
born

late 1820s
begins working

1849
escapes to Pennsylvania

1850s
leads people on Underground Railroad

The North and the South fought
the Civil War from 1861 to 1865.
Harriet was a nurse, a spy,
and a scout for the North.
The North won the war.
In December 1865, slavery
became illegal in all states.

1865

slavery becomes
illegal

1820s
born

late 1820s
begins working

1849
escapes to Pennsylvania

1850s
leads people on Underground Railroad

Harriet returned home to New York. She wanted to keep helping black people. She welcomed freed slaves and wounded black soldiers into her home. She helped black people who were old, sick, or homeless.

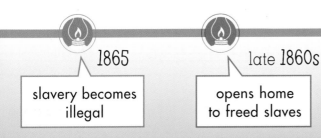

1865
slavery becomes illegal

late 1860s
opens home to freed slaves

1820s
born

late 1820s
begins working

1849
escapes to Pennsylvania

1850s
leads people on Underground Railroad

Remembering Harriet

Harriet died March 10, 1913.

People remember her for helping

slaves escape to freedom.

Harriet is also remembered for

helping freed slaves lead better lives.

1865
slavery becomes illegal

late 1860s
opens home to freed slaves

1913
dies

Glossary

Civil War—the U.S. war fought between the northern states and the southern states over slavery; the Civil War lasted from 1861 to 1865

escape—to break free from a place

illegal—against the law

safe house—a place where escaping slaves could hide; people who lived in these homes believed slavery was wrong

scout—someone sent to find and bring back information

slave—a person who is owned by another person; slaves are not free to choose their homes or jobs

spy—someone who secretly gathers information about an enemy

Underground Railroad—a series of safe houses and secret routes; many slaves escaped by traveling to the North from one house to another

Read More

Bauer, Marion Dane. *Harriet Tubman.* My First Biography. New York: Scholastic, 2010.

Bennett, Doraine. *Harriet Tubman.* American Heroes. Hamilton, Ga.: State Standards Pub., 2012.

Gosman, Gillian. *Harriet Tubman.* New York: PowerKids Press, 2011.

Internet Sites

FactHound offers a safe, fun way to find Internet sites related to this book. All of the sites on FactHound have been researched by our staff.

Here's all you do:

Visit *www.facthound.com*

Type in this code: 9781620650721

Check out projects, games and lots more at
www.capstonekids.com

Index

birth, 5
Civil War, 17
death, 21
escaping, 9, 11, 13, 15, 21
family, 5, 7, 11
freedom, 5, 21
nursing, 17

safe houses, 13
scouting, 17
slaves, 5, 7, 9, 13, 15, 19, 21
spying, 17
Underground Railroad, 13, 15

Word Count: 299
Grade: 1
Early-Intervention Level: 24

Editorial Credits
Erika L. Shores, editor; Alison Thiele, designer; Wanda Winch, media researcher; Jennifer Walker, production specialist

Photo Credits
Alamy Images: North Wind Picture Archives, 6, 8; Bridgeman Art Library/New York Public Library, USA, 1; Corbis: Bettmann, 14, National Geographic Society/Jerry Pinkney, 12; Janice Northcutt Huse, Artist, Port Charlotte, FL, 10; Library of Congress: Prints and Photographs Division, 4, 20; Shutterstock: Anton Novik, cover design; Super Stock Inc.: Culver Pictures Inc., cover, 18; Wikipedia, 16